The Orange Sky

Collection of poetry

Sheveta Singh

Copyright © Sheveta Singh

All Rights Reserved.

This book has been self-published with all reasonable efforts taken to make the material error-free by the author. No part of this book shall be used, reproduced in any manner whatsoever without written permission from the author, except in the case of brief quotations embodied in critical articles and reviews.

The Author of this book is solely responsible and liable for its content including but not limited to the views, representations, descriptions, statements, information, opinions, and references ["Content"]. The Content of this book shall not constitute or be construed or deemed to reflect the opinion or expression of the Publisher or Editor. Neither the Publisher nor Editor endorse or approve the Content of this book or guarantee the reliability, accuracy, or completeness of the Content published herein and do not make any representations or warranties of any kind, express or implied, including but not limited to the implied warranties of merchantability, fitness for a particular purpose.

The Publisher and Editor shall not be liable whatsoever...

Made with ❤ on the BookLeaf Publishing Platform

www.bookleafpub.in

www.bookleafpub.com

Dedication

For my Grandfather *Bishan Das Pakhetra*.
He was the Sun in our Winters.

Preface

The Poems in this book are outcome of the feel that was
more deeper than the ocean itself to me , just
like numerous beings incessantly flowing with one
thought after another. The world can never know what
sleeps inside the writers mind. But, then a Poem provides
that canvas where heart paints it's emotions. Here, it is
exactly the painting my HEART made when touched
with passion.

"Some of them are Authors of their own Scars".

Acknowledgements

I would like to express my deepest gratitude to my family and friends who have been the first readers of these poetry I created over the years. A special thanks to BookLeaf Publishing without which this dream would never have been breathing .

1. The Idol of the House

He was the Sun
An idol for one
Walking foot by foot
Causing hearts to arouse
Moved all to truth
Idolizing was
The Man of the house....

Tardy and with brains
All praised his strains
Little buds hid inside
Blossomed too were roused
Seeing his volcanic eyes
Idolizing was
The Man of the house....

No knowledge did remain
All in his gain
Cured that came weak
Pace with inner nous

Bribery did not seek
Idolizing was
The Man of the house....

An Epitome of love
A pair of dove
Shared all with half
Withered never his woes
He did never scoff
Idolizing was
The Man of the house....

Small garden he gained
With efforts it rained
Raised little with care
Never did they browse
Given all was fair
Idolizing was
The Man of the house....

Facing evil with difficulty
Escaping the pointed casuistry
He lived his rule
Keeping each small vows
Left with priestly soul
Idolizing was
The Man of the house.

2. REFORMATION

Falling down when child,
Bruises and cuts, did hurt
Playing, jumping, dancing
Sprains or scratches did hurt.
Crying loud in front of her,
Holding knees, tears with comfort.

Down on knees when wise,
Crying, crawling, sour eyes.
Bruised emotional ties,
Added up in core, secrets and lies.
Blood did not,
Its heart that cries.

3. An Unwitting Injury

5

The unrest and the wine
Drugs but not the Devine
Lust and the lustrous mind.

After the pleasure of organs,
The conscience goes blind.
Starving covetously with zeal,
Food may go but not figured meal.

Once killed was an Asura,
Of his desired deal.
Since then a voice gale-
Falls one when in lecher,
Never gets an ointment to heal.

4. Peeling Of The Fruit

Restricted in the edge, among
Those thousands stories, a
Maiden's story waited to be twisted.
"Here or there? Oh! That", yet a
Nakedness rested in to be drifted.

She shrugged at the thought,
Smiled to another layer.
Sensing soon a hand and
A voice near her ear.

"LOOK. The birds flying from
One tree to another branch.
To the corner, to that house.
You have wings too,
Lift your feet, for that rouse."

He moved a bit ahead her,
In his prints she stepped.
Air, the breeze, the trees grew warmly

Shedding behind thick sheets
Of her loved fruit calmly.

5. The Gone Needs

I never had you,
When I needed you,
I never had you,
Although, I needed you.

Roof of strength
over her I saw,
And me, looked up,
Could feel, no you.

Skinned knees of her,
With worried hands to cure,
And me skinned heart,
Could cure, no you.

Degree success of her,
With pair of happy tears,
And me holding degree,
No tears, no you.

Mistakes shuddered her,
To face the temper.
And me million mishaps,
Have no temper, no you.

Worlds great for her,
So great is him.
And me, world's against,
Still see me, no you.

I'll never have you.
When I'll need you
And I'll never have you
FATHER
Although, I need you.

6. THE UNLIT FIRE

So, out came the tear,
Umpteen, down to rosy lips.
Motioning the frozen ships,
In deepest of oceanic layer.
To and fro they sailed.
Some flown decade back,
Untangling every husky shack.
Mounts as black that jailed,
Enthralling into the darkest mere.
Tautened still firmly, that ailed.

One gaze and years slips,
Not with sweetest but saltiest sips.

7. Just In Dreams

Early in those days,
When I was a little fragile one
Starry eyed, simplistic under sun
I lived, loved, moved like insane
For the feeling of heart
And Lovely rain.
I sleeked, and reeked in emotions.
Flied high, not reading the caution.
How little did I know?
What I dreamt of, was just
A blue flame.
I was loved so sweetly,
Then, was left swiftly.
At times was a princess,
Sometimes named offensive.
When and where was I wrong?
In singing or dancing along
To their song.
I stayed behind and love moved,
Looking behind, straight in my eyes,

With a crude look.
Just in dreams, could I find
The perfect pair of Dove.
No rules, no tools
Like clouds flying above.

8. Death

If death could take me far.
Far from this guilt filled
World of mine.
If death could change.
Change what I am incapable
Of reverting.
If death for once could alter.
Alter your iced heart into
Water for me.
If death carried forgiveness.
Forgiveness for crushing your
Beliefs in me.
If death, my love, was an escape.
Escape into a new world
Where I'd wait for you.
If death, my dear one
Could give this all. I'd have
Embraced it in crave of
You ,yourself.

9. His or Her

Idols of His and Her
On the hills tops, nook stops.
In between the river they dwell,
With hopes, like ants admiration jell.
Hundreds shores, stairs, steps along swelling chests,
Loyalties here the only rest.
Inside or Out, the must to bend.
Idols of His and Her, a way to mend.

For this loyalty, immortality is all.
Around and round, big or small
If blue, its you guiding right shoe,
When black, you are glinting rest to soul.
Pure or pale, for existence, I fend
Idols of His or Her, for others to bend.

10. Lets take some rest....

Lets take some rest
The words can wait
Pages, the knowledge,
The world can update.

The sages, the foretellers,
the Predictions they made.
Lazy and Laziness,
Slumber has its weight.

Tales listed in evidence,
LIONS sleep its hours,
DONKEYS works straight
still King's not afraid.

Dreams, as infant crops,
Waver in empty brains
Take some time,
Move bit from sprains.

Saying - "Work, come tomorrow",
No, never is OWL.
As for me -
The world can upgrade
Lets rest , why wait.

11. Fairy Tale

A fairy tale, that didn't exist.
Became a saddest poetry, in some lost list.
A beauty, with no loving beast,
A Cinderella, with no charming Prince.
A beauty, left to sleep forever,
Deprived of true lover's kiss.
A helpless mermaid, washed off from shores,
Isolated, in tower of her own thoughts.
A tale, that when suffered the most,
Found itself alone,
With no caring soul.
Except, the Immortal, That decided its roles.

12. The Ladder to Success

Arise, Awake, And move forth.
Know that, You exist not just to woe Man,
But are a women of high worth.
The womb to create universe,
You carry by birth.

Soft hearted, the healer as you are,
Stand only beside the virtuous ladder,
That could help you meet, the need of an hour.

In build the valour, to step forward.
Whether born or not, with gifted wings,
Strengthen your muscles, to hold the ladder hard.
Gain Autonomy to freely climb up.
Earn, to rise above.

13. Heartless

Out it came at times
The pain, the pinch in chest
Just as the heart was ready to set

She didn't know the reason
Why everything gets frozen ?
Even, after dancing like chimes

Alas ! She was never viewed
The previous birth...
Of Rose and Nightingale worth

How she then sang
Gushing her blood into love
Impressing the mighty Jove

Their she was born again
With the Thorn's unrest
To give, not to gain the nest

14. A SIN

Far, somewhere,
Just behind those fluffy clouds,
God sat to look
At the world of doubts.
Some, got love. Some, cried for love.

God smiled and rubbed his hands.
Thus, creating a mist with wands.
"Love is thee, Love it be
The Gift, the treasure for Ye."

The month she was born,
Hour too stooped to see,
A girl of Love
God had made with glee.

Far, somewhere between those years,
She visioned her gift of LOVE.
She didn't keep it but,
Shared with whole.

"It's sane." God words glared to get the win.
But down there on land,
People called it ," A SIN."

15. Just Another News

Young Reha saw
different years pass by....
Different seasons and tastes of water.
One place to other,
One hand to another,
Little did she remember her mother.
But how could she ever forget...
Eyes that bargained her.

Her heart rained,
When those fingers rolled,
Rusted bodies crawled over her.
She wondered, if world was alike.
Then she gained,
Gained to learn her busted fate.

Was she cursed
Or were those demons?
Who cheated her, rated her...
Why was not she free?

Free to walk, to talk.
She travelled, she walked,
on the same roads.
But those eyes, many of them chained her.

She cried...cried hard.
If there was God,
Was Devil too strong ?
No Potent she believed in
Her destiny was retard.

Young Reha saw
She Saw one day...
deep down the river flowed,
"Free she could be." She thought.
With open hands , She threw her fate.
How free she was, no one could ever rate.

Drowned insanely her meat
Many a times that became a devil's treat.
No use, yet another News,
A young girl named REHA
"Once lost from arms, lost
again with ravished charms."

16. The Beach

The long sandy beach
waves of deep blue water
and she standing alone
Her hair touched her face
but today, no eyes to stare

The long sandy beach
the very same place
when she had reached
her hair touched her face
with those Eyes to stare

Deep blue waves
made it realize
the past, the remembrance
and she standing alone

Her hands got numb
sitting on her knees
she stared at the long beach

where once she wasn't alone

25

17. Protector

Several times, I
Uttered your name.
Numbered, outnumbered fame.
Nothing was still inside,
Yet I climbed the tide.
On the top when I reached,
My hands touched thy feet.
Seconds later I fell deep,
Under the ravenous sea.
Not knowing what it was,
Numbed body flowed with waves.
Yelled again my heart the name.
Out I stretched my hand in vain.
Moments ended the storm with rain.

18. Foreign Land

In search of something beautiful,
I once entered into a huddled land.
More enchanting than the real world
Vibrant, lively like the precious gold.

Moving in , and much inside
I saw faces with only lovely side.
What was real? What was fake?
All minds were blinded for diamonds sake.

There was greenery all around
Words only spoke with sweet sound
I ran up and down into that ground
Far, even farther from the world of wound.

A day came, when I reached a place
Although false but with tempted solace.
I first halted, and then stepped over.
An alluring scent, out came through a blower.

On the left I saw an existing door
Shining mirror reflecting my soul.
Struggling hard I reached there
Was sucked back, for my fate read.

The door bared bmy true land
Me stuck but outside was grand.
Falsely I played my plan,
Once told by rose of high stand.

Stealthily I clutched the knob
Pulled open, dumping sparkly robe
A tenderness caressed me.
I too embraced back a new hope.

19. Beloved

A soul prayed, praised the Pious
In return gained the desires.
Warm honey stored in nowhere,
Only you and I knew the way to there.

Like waterfall upside down,
Blood rushed in veins.
And You, my love too in chains.

Same as a dew drop,
I sleep in your eyes, only
to fly when dawn arrives.
An impression Sun makes on water,
Enjoys, then soon dries.
Silk movement of river over stones,
Is Us, feeling its song.
The sky, the mountains never meet,
But alone are incomplete.

Although, the physique know

They are far, even apart.
The nature, the solicit soul,
Will ever after show us in one Part.

20. Embrace

Blossomed inside the chest
Like a rose in its green plant
Warm cheeks blushing best
Just as raindrops on icy slant
Locking up of arms
Gushing in and out lives
Mutually brought together charms
As after touching moon, sea dives

Blest those with esteem
Day to night endlessly dream

21. The Last Note

Before you ask her to leave,
She herself would flee.
Into that deep blue sea,
Where no one, but she could be.

Just before she decide to flee,
A little note, a kiss to sweet ache,
Hug to his presence, tearful leave she'll take.

Before you say "Goodbye",
And she could avoid asking "Why?"
A step above she'll try,
To add yet another name,
Written on sky, to fly.

www.ingramcontent.com/pod-product-compliance
Lightning Source LLC
La Vergne TN
LVHW010931200726

843509LV00013B/2168